REDEEMED

HOW GOD SATISFIES
the LONGING SOUL

STUDY GUIDE | FIVE SESSIONS

WILL GRAHAM

with Erik Ogren

Thomas Nelson
Since 1798

Redeemed Study Guide

© 2019 by William F. Graham IV

Published in Nashville, Tennessee, by Thomas Nelson. Thomas Nelson is a registered trademark of HarperCollins Christian Publishing, Inc.

Billy Graham quotes taken from previously published material in *Billy Graham in Quotes* and used by permission of the Billy Graham Evangelistic Association.

All Scripture quotations, unless otherwise indicated, are taken from The New King James Version®. Copyright © 1982 by Thomas Nelson. Used by permission. All rights reserved.

Thomas Nelson titles may be purchased in bulk for educational, business, fund-raising, or sales promotional use. For information, please e-mail SpecialMarkets@ ThomasNelson.com.

ISBN 978-0-310-09976-5

First Printing March 2019 / Printed in the United States of America

Contents

———◇◇———

INTRODUCTION

———◦◦◦———

*M*y friend, there is no one out there quite like you. The way you look, the way you act, the way you believe, the things you say, your innermost thoughts . . . there are so many things that make you unique. As David says, you are "fearfully and wonderfully made," knit together by God (Psalm 139:14). Before you were even born, your heavenly Father had a plan and a purpose just for you. You are special. You are His handiwork.

In other ways, however, I imagine that you are similar to most people on the planet.

I've had the opportunity to travel the globe, preaching across six of the seven continents. I've shared the hope of Jesus in massive stadiums in world-class cities, in small Australian outback towns, and in Himalayan villages. I've ministered in the foothills of Mount Kilimanjaro and north of the Arctic Circle. In doing so, I've met people from countless different cultures and walks of life.

Throughout my journeys, I have come to realize that—even though we are each very unique—we also share many of the same basic needs and desires. Of course, we need food, water, air, and shelter, but I'm talking about something less physical and much deeper. I'm talking about a spiritual hunger that comes from the depths of our souls.

We all feel the need for love and acceptance. We all desire hope and peace. We all seek purpose, safety, and fulfillment.

Everywhere you look, including in your church today, people are trying to fill these needs in their own power. They seek to satisfy the hunger through relationships, family, work, or hobbies. They fill their garage with cars and their homes with possessions. They may invest everything they have in philanthropic endeavors or serving others. Sadly, some even seek fulfillment in destructive behaviors that not only fail to fill the void but also leave them far worse than when they started.

No matter what we try, however, it can't fill that hole. Nothing we do can bring true happiness or peace. None of our individual efforts result in lasting hope. We strive, we struggle, we plead, we fight—and yet the hunger remains.

When I began writing my book *Redeemed*, my pastor shared a message out of Psalm 107. That passage—especially verse 9—stuck with me. It caught me in a way that it had not before. I filed it away and pondered it for some time.

Months later, as we were wrapping up the manuscript, my assistant was leading devotions for our team at the Billy Graham Training Center at The Cove in Asheville, North Carolina, and she shared Psalm 107:9—the exact same verse that I had been contemplating. I quickly realized it was not a coincidence that the verse bookended my writing. God was speaking to me and wanting me to share this very simple message:

> *For He satisfies the longing soul, and fills*
> *the hungry soul with goodness.*

That short verse is so straightforward that many would be tempted to fly right past it, and yet it is entirely profound! Everything we search for—all those elements the world finds so elusive—are found in Christ and Him alone!

He is the One who satisfies the deep longing of our soul. He fills that empty void with His goodness. It's not more stuff. It's not more work. It's not harmful vices. It's Jesus!

My grandfather once said there's a God-shaped hole in each of us, and none of our vain efforts can fill it. Only Christ—as we call upon Him and are redeemed—can fill that deep longing in our soul.

As we begin this study together, I hope you will be inspired to let go of your past and embrace the new life that Christ has for you as a child of the King. I pray that you will begin to realize His purpose for you and that you will be challenged to share with others that same peace, hope, and love you have found in Him.

Most of all, in the coming weeks, I pray that your longing soul will be filled with the goodness of the Father.

How to Use
THIS GUIDE

⸻∞⸻

*T*he *Redeemed Video Study* is designed to be experienced in a group setting such as a Bible study, Sunday school class, or any small group gathering. Each session begins with a brief welcome section and several opening questions to get you thinking about the topic. You will then watch a video with Will Graham and jump into some directed small-group discussion. You will close each session with a time of prayer and personal reflection.

To get the most out of your group experience, keep the following points in mind. First, the real growth in this study will happen during your small-group time. This is where you will process the content of the teaching for the week, ask questions, and learn from others as you hear what God is doing in their lives. For this reason, it is important for you to be fully committed to the group and attend each session so you can build trust and rapport with the other members. If you choose to only "go through the motions," or if you refrain from participating, there is a lesser chance you will find what you're looking for during this study.

Second, remember the goal of your small group is to serve as a place where people can share, learn about God, and build intimacy and friendship. For this reason, seek to make your group a "safe place." This means being honest about your thoughts and feelings and listening carefully to everyone else's opinion. (If you are a group leader, there are additional instructions and resources in the back of the book for leading a productive discussion group.)

Third, resist the temptation to "fix" a problem someone might be having or to correct his or her theology, as that's not the purpose of your small-group time. Also, keep everything your group shares confidential. This will foster a rewarding sense of community in your group and create a place where people can heal, be challenged, and grow spiritually.

Following your group time, reflect on the material you've covered by engaging in any or all of the between-sessions activities. For each session, you may wish to complete the personal study all in one sitting or spread it out over a few days (for example, working on it a half-hour a day on different days that week). Note that if you are unable to finish (or even start!) your between-sessions personal study, you should still attend the group study video session. You are still wanted and welcome at the group even if you don't have your "homework" done.

Keep in mind the videos, discussion questions, and activities are simply meant to kick-start your imagination so you are not only open to what God wants you to hear but also how to apply it to your life. As Jesus promised, "Ask, and it will be given to you; seek, and you will find; knock, and it will be opened to you." So ask, seek, and knock . . . and then listen to what the Lord is saying to you about being a *redeemed* child of God.

Note: *If you are a group leader, there are additional resources provided in the back of this guide to help you lead your group members through the study.*

SESSION
One

A New Understanding of God's Love

———❖———

Your salvation depends on what
[Christ] has done for you, not
on what you can do for Him.
It isn't your hold on God that
saves you; it's His hold on you.
BILLY GRAHAM

———❖———

WELCOME

"Jesus loves me, this I know, for the Bible tells me so . . ."

From our earliest years, many of us have known of the love that God has for us. The words roll freely from our lips as we discuss our faith or consider our relationship with Him.

However, for a variety of reasons, some of us today may doubt that love.

For instance, a friend once told me that because he never knew his earthly father, it was hard for him to understand there could be a heavenly Father who loved him. Though he could understand it intellectually, he was unable to fully appreciate it emotionally and spiritually.

Perhaps you're going through a difficult time in your family or your marriage. A loved one has repeatedly told you that you are worthless, and it's getting harder and harder to believe there's a God out there who loves you unconditionally.

Or maybe you may feel you've gone too far down the wrong road, and there's no way that God could love you. You haven't earned it, and you don't deserve it. His unconditional love may be great for others, but it's not so unconditional as to be reserved for you.

Or maybe you've been in the church for so long that discussing the love of God is like talking about dinner plans. It's just something that's a part of your daily routine. Similar to an inoculation, you've gotten a large enough dose that it simply doesn't affect you anymore.

If you have watched any of my grandfather's old crusade sermons, you've likely heard him say, "If you take nothing else from tonight, know this: God loves you! God loves you! God . . . loves . . . you!"

Whatever your circumstances today, I'm here to tell you the same thing. *God loves you!* He loves you with an overarching, eternal love, and He's waiting to embrace you today.

SHARE

If you or any of your group members are just getting to know one another, take a few minutes to introduce yourselves. Then, to kick things off, discuss one of the following questions:

- How do people in your family (or circle of friends) show love to each other? What does love look like for you?

– or –

- Why did you choose to take part in this study? What are you hoping to get out of this time together?

READ

Invite someone to read aloud the following passage. Listen for fresh insights as you hear the verses being read, and then discuss the questions that follow.

As the Father loved Me, I also have loved you; abide in My love. If you keep My commandments, you will abide in My love, just as I have kept My Father's commandments and abide in His love. These things I have spoken to you, that My joy may remain in you, and that your joy may be full. This is My commandment, that you love one another as I have loved you. Greater love has no one than this, than to lay down one's life for his friends (John 15:9–13).

What do you think it means to abide in God's love?

How does the love of God help us to be filled with joy?

Have you ever considered that you should love others as Christ has loved you? Is that love reserved just for your friends and family, or for everybody you encounter?

WATCH

Play the video segment for session one. As you watch, use the following outline to record any thoughts or concepts that stand out to you.

NOTES

I believe that the Creator of the universe knows my name. He knows my tears and pain. He knows my triumphs and struggles. Through it all, He loves me.

Like my grandfather's embrace, God loves me with an eternal, unconditional love. He loves me so much that He gave His Son to die for me.

When you consider the sacrifice of Christ from the perspective of a parent who longs to protect and love his or her child above all else, you can begin to understand the pain that was felt not only by Jesus at His crucifixion, but by God the Father as well.

God's all-encompassing love—as evidenced through the sacrifice and resurrection of Jesus—is for each of us. Regardless of who you are or what you've done. Christ took your sins to the cross and subsequently conquered the grave. Now we can have eternal hope in Him.

It doesn't matter how good you are. It doesn't matter who you are. A relationship with Christ—accepting the love that He offers—is what secures your eternity with Him in heaven, and brings a lifetime of joy, peace, and purpose in this world.

Once you've found and embraced the love of God, you must pass it on to others by serving them and sharing the hope that is within you.

God's Word says that "faith comes by hearing" (Romans 10:17). It also promises that when the time comes, God will give you the words to say as you share that love with those around you (see Luke 12:12).

DISCUSS

Take a few minutes with your group members to discuss what you just watched and explore these concepts together.

1. When I was a child, I had direct access to my grandfather because I was his grandson. I was part of his family, so I could go directly to him and fall into his embrace. Does this describe the way you feel about the access you have to God? Why or why not?

2. Some people struggle with the idea that God loves them, while others have heard it so often they take it for granted. Where do you fall on that spectrum? How can you begin to genuinely understand and appreciate the love that God freely gives?

3. Have you considered Christ's sacrifice on the cross through the lens of God as a Father who sent His child to die for the sake of others? If you are a parent, how does the love you have for your own children impact your understanding of God's love for you?

4. My father shared the love of Jesus with me on that day I tried to take part in communion at our church. He explained to me that I needed to invite Jesus into my life and forgive me of my sin. Who are the people in your world who need to hear that same message? What can you do to share the gospel with them?

5. Jesus' love for you was sacrificial. He was beaten, spat upon, mocked, and tortured because of the depth of His affection for you. While you don't need to go to that extreme, what are some ways you can sacrificially show love to those around you?

6. The Bible says the Holy Spirit will give you the words to say when you have opportunities to share the love of God with others. Have you found that to be true? If you've never shared the gospel with those around you, what's holding you back?

PRAY

Wrap up your time together by taking a few minutes to talk with God. Here are a few ideas of what you could pray about based on what you discussed in this session:

- Thank God for His sacrificial love for you—love undeserved but freely given.
- Ask God to soften your heart so you can begin to fully realize and understand the depth of His love for you.
- Renew your commitment to God as your loving Father.
- Ask God to wrap you in His embrace, allowing you to feel His presence and love in your life.
- Ask God to show you others who need to hear of this love and for boldness to share that message when given the opportunity.

RESPOND

This week, I invite you to take time to consider God's love for you. First, do a spiritual status check. Have you surrendered your past, present, and future into Jesus' hands as your Savior and Lord? If not, don't waste another minute! Perhaps, like the story of the prodigal son told in Luke 15:11–32, you've been wandering away from the Father. Come home! It's only when you've taken that step that you can truly experience the love that awaits you as a child of God. Once you have, the Holy Spirit will begin opening doors for you to take that love and pass it on to others who desperately need it. Be ready for those opportunities!

Between-Sessions
PERSONAL STUDY

———◇∞◇———

A big part of growing in your knowledge and understanding of God's love is spending time daily with Him. Just like a person-to-person relationship requires time, commitment, and development, so your relationship with Jesus will grow deeper as you dwell in His presence. So, reflect on the material you've covered this week by engaging in any or all of the following between-sessions activities. Each day offers a short reading adapted from my book *Redeemed*, along with a few reflection questions to take you deeper into the theme of this week's study. I encourage you to journal or jot down your thoughts if you'd like. At the start of the next session, you will have a few minutes to share any insights you learned . . . but remember, the primary goal of these questions is for your own spiritual growth and private reflection.

— *Day One* —

A SOFT ANSWER TURNS
AWAY WRATH, BUT A HARSH
WORD STIRS UP ANGER.
PROVERBS 15:1

A few decades ago, my grandfather was invited to speak at the inauguration ceremony of a seminary president. This particular meeting promised to be controversial. The incoming president would be leading the seminary back to a more traditional, conservative theology, and this wasn't a particularly popular stance with some faculty.

When my grandfather arrived, he was amazed to find that faculty lined both sides of the walkway leading up to where the induction would be held. My grandfather was so moved by the display that he graciously shook hands and greeted every person along the way. He couldn't have envisioned a greater welcome and outpouring of love.

Later, my grandfather exclaimed to the incoming president, "I can't believe they all came out to greet me!"

"Billy," the president responded. "They weren't here to greet you! They were here to protest you!"

I love how God works. My grandfather was a sweet, thoughtful, loving person, who genuinely and deeply cared about others, even if they disagreed with him. In this case, God used my grandfather's naivety to break down walls of anger and hurt, opening the door for reconciliation and healing amid a potentially explosive situation.

My grandfather graciously—if naively—greeted every person who was there to protest him. What kind of impact do you think that expression of love may have had on the people who were there for the purpose of being confrontational?

How do you tend to respond in difficult or negative situations? What is the impact you have seen of showing grace and love in the midst of trying times?

How can you show love today to people who may be confrontational or rude to you?

In difficult (or even mundane) situations, have you ever prayed, "God, help me to love people like you love people"? How might that change your outlook regarding those around you?

— *Day Two* —

THROUGH THE LORD'S MERCIES WE ARE NOT
CONSUMED, BECAUSE HIS COMPASSIONS
FAIL NOT. THEY ARE NEW EVERY MORNING;
GREAT IS YOUR FAITHFULNESS.
LAMENTATIONS 3:22–23

Several years ago, a lady came up to me following a sermon. "You look just like your grandfather, Billy Graham," she proclaimed.

"Oh," I laughed. "You mean I have a big mouth, big nose and big ears."

She earnestly agreed, "Yeah! You do!"

I'll admit that I had a little fun with this sweet lady. But the fact of the matter is that it is an incredible honor whenever someone mentions he and I in the same sentence. It's humbling when people witness some of his characteristics in me. Whether it's the North Carolina accent, the way I move my hands as I speak, or certain turns of phrase that I've picked up over the years, as the grandson of Billy Graham, I model some of his traits. It's inevitable.

You likely model some of the same looks and behaviors of your parents and grandparents as well. And just as people can see a glimpse of my grandfather in me, and perhaps yours in you, they should also be able to look at you and see that you exemplify the attributes of your heavenly Father.

In good times and bad, we should all be merciful, compassionate, and faithful. We would do well to exhibit holiness, love, grace, forgiveness, and righteousness.

Do you exhibit any family traits that you've inherited from your parents or grandparents? If so, what are those traits?

What characteristics of God do you feel most closely exemplify your walk with Him? Are there any you need to work on?

Jeremiah wrote the words of Lamentations 3:22–23 during a disastrous, painful circumstance. Do you tend to draw closer to God when faced with a difficult situation? If so, why?

What does it mean to conduct yourself in a way that is fitting for an heir of your heavenly Father? How could that impact your actions today as you share His love with others?

— *Day Three* —

BE STILL, AND KNOW THAT I AM GOD;
I WILL BE EXALTED AMONG THE NATIONS,
I WILL BE EXALTED IN THE EARTH!

PSALM 46:10

During the last few years of his life, as I sat with my grandfather, there was very little talk on either side. For the most part, we spent our time simply being together. Words didn't need to be spoken. We could just rest in the presence of one another.

Similarly, I believe it's vital to rest in the presence of God. Life is so hectic—schedules that are full morning until evening, jobs to do, bills to pay, phones that never stop chiming, and relationships that require ongoing development and attention.

These aren't necessarily bad things, but it can be difficult to tap the brakes and slow down when we try to spend quiet time with God. We'll race through a short passage of Scripture and our list of prayer requests, keeping one eye on the phone to make sure we don't miss that text.

My friends, I encourage you to meditate on the words of Psalm 46:10: "Be still, and know that I am God." As you do, you'll find the stress of the world diminishing in the hopeful peace of the One who saves. And you may discover that He uses that time to provide answers to the difficult questions in your life.

Why is it so hard to simply rest in the presence of God?

As a child of God, have you ever considered how much it must please Him for you to come into His presence? How do you tend to picture how God reacts when you come into His presence?

How could resting in God's presence help you to carry His love with you and possibly even share it with others?

What tangible things can you do to shut out the world for a time so you can focus solely on Jesus Christ and His love for you?

— *Day Four* —

> HAVING RECEIVED THE PIECE OF
> BREAD, [JUDAS] THEN WENT OUT
> IMMEDIATELY. AND IT WAS NIGHT.
>
> JOHN 13:30

One thing my life as a traveling evangelist has taught me is that loneliness is one of the most prevalent human conditions, regardless of country or culture. However, the loneliness I see most often is a *longing for God*. It's that empty spiritual cavern inside that will only be filled when the longing soul calls upon Him as Savior.

There's a powerful passage of Scripture found in the Gospel of John that I believe speaks directly to this matter of loneliness and being apart from the Lord. Jesus had just announced that Judas would betray Him, and Judas—now separated from fellowship—walked outside.

John then says the simple phrase, "And it was night." Those four words are literal and figurative. Yes, it was nighttime, but that narrative also describes Judas' soul as he walked away from the Savior. Spiritually speaking, it was dark and it was lonely.

Perhaps that describes your world right now. You want to live in the light, but you know that you're far from God. In your faith journey, it is night. If that's the case, there's one remedy, and it's drawing close to God. He's right there with you, waiting for you to turn to Him.

Do you struggle with loneliness? Why or why not?

When are you loneliest? When you're all by yourself or when you're in a room filled with people? Explain.

In the passage from John, we are told that it was night—a dark, cold, lonely place. Have you ever been in that place spiritually? Are you there now?

As you contemplate God's sacrificial love for you, understand that He doesn't want you to stay in that dark place. He's waiting for you to draw near to Him. How will you begin to do that in the coming days? How will you step from the darkness into the light of Christ?

— Day Five —

THOSE WHO SOW IN TEARS

SHALL REAP IN JOY.

PSALM 126:5

More than 100 years ago, my great-grandparents arrived in China as medical missionaries. My great-grandparents loved the Chinese people. They sacrificed greatly to serve in the name of Jesus, even though the ministry wasn't always fruitful.

A few years ago, I had the great honor of visiting Huai'an in China to share the gospel. Planning to preach from John 3:16, I had discovered a decades-old video recording of my great-grandfather reading that passage in Huai'anese.

As my great-grandfather's recorded voice crackled forth, I heard a chorus of small gasps. The eyes of the 3,000 who had crammed into the church sparkled. I could see the love that they had for my family. In that moment, I was overcome by tears.

Many surrendered their lives to Jesus that day, and I felt I was harvesting a field that I did not sow. It was only because of the love and sacrifice of my great-grandparents a century ago that many were now claiming the hope of the Savior.

I'm sure my great-grandparents spent countless hours on their knees, crying out to God for the souls of the Huai'anese people. I would encourage you to do the same for those in your life who need Jesus. Those who sow in tears shall reap in joy!

When was the last time you cried out to God on behalf of someone? Did He answer your plea?

My great-grandparents loved (and sacrificed for) the people of China because God first loved them. While we aren't all called to be international missionaries, how has God's love compelled you to love others?

Are you passionate about the gospel to the point of shedding tears over the lost people around you? Why or why not?

The passage my great-grandfather read, John 3:16, speaks to the eternal love of Jesus. Take a few minutes to ponder that verse, inserting your name into it as you consider the sacrifice offered in order to show His love for you and redeem your soul.

For God so loved _____ that He gave His only begotten Son, that if _____ believes in Him, _____ should not perish but have everlasting life.

My friend, that is how much God loves you!

A New Freedom from the Past

⎯⎯⎯◇◇◇⎯⎯⎯

BECAUSE OF WHAT JESUS CHRIST DID
FOR US THROUGH HIS CROSS AND
RESURRECTION, WE KNOW THAT WE
HAVE HOPE FOR THE FUTURE.

BILLY GRAHAM

⎯⎯⎯◇◇◇⎯⎯⎯

WELCOME

People often ask me if I ever went through a rebellious stage in my life, and I can honestly say that I didn't. I was a good kid, and I believe that God spared me a lot of heartache because of that.

That doesn't mean, however, that I was perfect. No, far from it! I was mischievous, and my brothers and I would get into trouble as we ran through the mountains of the small town of Boone, North Carolina. We weren't intentionally bad, but we probably caused a few headaches.

I do recall one time when I really messed up. My mom took me to a general store that had open barrels of candy. You were supposed to scoop the candy into plastic bags and then pay by the pound. On that particular day, when no one was looking, I reached into the barrel and stole candy. I took something that didn't belong to me and didn't pay for it.

You can bet that when my mom found out about this, I was in serious trouble! She took me right back down to the store, and I had to acknowledge my indiscretion, pay for the candy, and ask for forgiveness. Looking back, I'm glad that she handled the situation the way she did. I'm sure it wasn't easy for her either, but I learned a valuable lesson.

You see, I was a comparatively good kid, but I was still a sinner. That is the case for all of us. We're in church, we follow the Lord, we tithe, we do great things in our community . . . but ultimately, we're all still sinners. In fact, Paul tells us in

Romans 3:23 that we all have fallen short of the glory—the perfection—of God.

The problem is, we live in an age where sin is no longer something to be *repented* of but something to be *celebrated*. Ours is such a sin-soaked culture that many of us don't even know what the word means anymore. There are even many Christians who will say, "What's the big deal? I'm forgiven."

My friends, as we'll see today, sin is a big deal. It has real life-and-death consequences and is not something to be taken lightly. However, we serve a Savior who is bigger than the sin in our lives—and who is ready to forgive us if we give our brokenness over to Him.

SHARE

If you or any of your group members are just getting to know one another, take a few minutes to introduce yourselves and share any insights you have from last week's personal study. As you begin this week's study, discuss one of the following questions:

- I stole candy when I was young. What was your childhood indiscretion? Can you remember the first time you realized you had done something wrong?

— *or* —

- Have you ever messed up but received a pardon or forgiveness? How did that make you feel?

READ

Invite someone to read aloud the following passage. Listen for fresh insights as you hear the verses being read, and then discuss the questions that follow.

> *Then Jesus spoke to them again, saying, "I am the light of the world. He who follows Me shall not walk in darkness, but have the light of life" (John 8:12).*

What do you think it means to "walk in darkness"?

Consider the stark difference between spiritual light and spiritual darkness. How would you relate that to the world you live in today—a world in which many believe there is no right or wrong?

What would your daily routine look like if you could constantly reside in the "light of life"?

WATCH

Play the video for session two. As you and your group watch, use the following outline to record any thoughts or key points that stand out to you.

Notes

Many people believe they've gone too far down the wrong road and there's no way God could ever love them . . . let alone save them. But God is bigger than our sins and our past. He paid the price for those very sins that are causing us so much heartache.

Although we've all sinned, that doesn't make it okay to sin. Sin is a real problem with real consequences.

What are the consequences of sin?

- Sin separates us from God, building a barrier that stands between us and Him.

- Sin claims us as its victim.

- Sin causes us to become spiritually blind.

- Sin draws us into open rebellion against God.

But there is hope! Jesus conquered not only sin but the grave as well. Because of that, we can have freedom from the sin that binds us.

We can't be good enough to get to heaven, and there's nothing we can do to earn forgiveness and the gift of salvation, but God made another way.

Jesus came on a rescue mission. Knowing that God could not have sin in His holy presence, Jesus humbled Himself and became man, paid the price of our sin, and conquered the grave. He created a way for us—broken as we are—to find eternity with a perfect and blameless God.

God doesn't want to put a band-aid on our brokenness. He wants to give us a whole new life, free of the pain we're carrying.

DISCUSS

As we move to the discussion time, I want to make one thing clear. Each of you—like me—is a sinner. We've all messed up and sinned against God. I don't want you to feel like you need to share everything wrong you've ever done, but I also don't want you to put up a front and pretend you're perfect. Rather, take an honest look at your own life and how Christ has offered you a new freedom from the past. Now, with that said, spend a few minutes with your group members, discussing what you just watched and exploring these concepts together.

1. We live in a society that celebrates sin rather than repents of it. What is your view of sin? Do you consider it harmful or just another part of your day? Explain.

2. Many people—particularly non-believers, but some Christians as well—view sin as inconsequential. What are some of the negative consequences you have suffered in the past because of your sinful actions?

3. Was there a time in your life when you—like Catherine in one of the stories I told—felt you had gone too far down the wrong road and there was no way Jesus could love, accept, or forgive you? Do you still feel that way? If not, what changed?

4. Sin builds a barrier between us and God. When we're stuck in a pattern of sinfulness, it's like trying to talk to a friend through a wall. Have you ever experienced this? What was it like for you? Conversely, what is it like when you spend concerted time focusing on the Bible and prayer?

5. God is holy and perfect, and sin cannot exist in His presence. Each of us—on the other hand—are covered in the filth of our sins. So how can a sinful person enter into the eternal presence of a blameless God?

6. Jesus paid the penalty for our sins so we can enter into His holy presence. However, we also must surrender our lives to Him, repent, and seek forgiveness for those sins. What do you think Jesus meant when He said, "I am the way, the truth, and the life. No one comes to the Father except through Me" (John 14:6)?

PRAY

Wrap up your time together by taking a few minutes to talk with God. Consider the points below as you seek the Savior in prayer.

- In the silence, examine your own walk with God and any areas where sinfulness has become deeply rooted in your life. Allow the Holy Spirit to convict you where needed.
- Ask God for forgiveness and for His divine help in turning away from those sins.

- Understanding that we're all sinners, pray for one another and the burdens or struggles that each person is carrying.
- Jesus' death on the cross and victory over sin and the grave have allowed us to have a new freedom from the past. Thank Him for this incredible sacrifice and gift.
- Commit to walking in the "light of life" as a follower of Jesus.

RESPOND

I get it . . . we all like to put up strong fronts, especially at church. We dress nicely. We smile. We answer joyously when someone asks how we're doing. Our reality, however, can be quite different. Life is messy, broken. Perhaps you're the kind of person who manages to keep his or her struggles hidden behind closed doors. Maybe your issues have been more public, and the consequences you've reaped are an open book. Either way, consider that your sins are potentially holding you back from experiencing true freedom in Christ. Peace can be found by openly acknowledging your sin and laying it at the foot of the cross. Below you will find three lines on which you can privately record your struggles, followed by the words of a wonderful old hymn. I encourage you to truly surrender it all to Jesus.

1. _____

2. _____

3. _____

ALL TO JESUS I SURRENDER

Winfield S. Weeden and
Judson W. Van DeVenter

All to Jesus I surrender,
All to Him I freely give;
I will ever love and trust Him,
In His presence daily live.

I surrender all,
I surrender all.
All to Thee, my blessed Savior,
I surrender all.

All to Jesus I surrender,
Humbly at His feet I bow,
Worldly pleasures all forsaken;
Take me, Jesus, take me now.

All to Jesus I surrender,
Make me, Savior, wholly Thine;
Let me feel Thy Holy Spirit,
Truly know that Thou art mine.

All to Jesus I surrender,
Lord, I give myself to Thee;
Fill me with Thy love and power,
Let Thy blessing fall on me.

All to Jesus I surrender,
Now I feel the sacred flame.
Oh, the joy of full salvation!
Glory, glory to His name.

Between-Sessions
PERSONAL STUDY

This week, you and your group discussed a new freedom from the past—how Jesus has redeemed you and how the sin that once held you captive has been conquered by Christ's sacrifice and victory over the grave. As you work through this week's personal study, remember that sin and death have lost their sting and sway. You are a loved and redeemed child of God who has been set free! I encourage you to journal or write down your thoughts if you would like. Feel free to share any observations with the group next week, but remember, the primary goal of these questions is for your own spiritual growth and private reflection.

— *Day One* —

FOR THE WAGES OF SIN IS DEATH,
BUT THE GIFT OF GOD IS ETERNAL
LIFE IN CHRIST JESUS OUR LORD.
ROMANS 6:23

I didn't even realize I was speeding until I saw the flashing lights. I handed the officer my license and acknowledged my mistake. Thankfully, he let me go with a warning rather than issuing me a ticket. "Thank you for your grace," I said to him.

"You know, that's exactly what this is," he replied. With that, he walked back to his car and drove away.

As I ponder that encounter, I view it through the lens of my faith and the gift of God. I've broken God's laws, and—in this case—the laws of man. And yet, by Christ's sacrifice and forgiveness, that sin has been taken away from me.

As I think back to that day, I realized I said *grace* to the officer, but what I really meant was *mercy*. Grace is getting what you don't deserve. Mercy is not getting what you do deserve. At that moment, I deserved a speeding ticket. Likewise, in my life, I deserve punishment for my sin. But thankfully, I've placed my hope in the hands of a Savior who offers mercy and grace!

Grace and mercy are two separate things, but they go hand in hand. I'm eternally thankful that I serve a Savior who freely offers both as I call on His name.

Have you ever had a similar experience where you've been released with a warning when you should have received a ticket? If so, how did that encounter make you feel?

In your view, what's the difference between grace and mercy? Why do we need both?

The first half of Romans 6:23—"for the wages of sin"—is an eternal death sentence. How does the second half—"the gift of God is eternal life"—represent the hope of the gospel?

The police officer offered me mercy but also acknowledged my disobedience. How does this anecdote parallel your repentance of sin as you come before God in prayer?

— Day Two —

AND ONE OF THEM, WHEN HE SAW THAT HE
WAS HEALED, RETURNED, AND WITH A LOUD
VOICE GLORIFIED GOD, AND FELL DOWN ON HIS
FACE AT HIS FEET, GIVING HIM THANKS.

LUKE 17:15–16

One of my favorite parts of an evangelistic crusade comes after the evening's events are over. That may seem like an odd time to label as one of my favorites, but it's true. Why? Because it's when we give thanks.

In Luke 17, we see the story of ten men who were afflicted by leprosy. They were not only suffering the physical toll of the disease but also being shunned as societal outcasts. Jesus entered the city, heard their pleas, and told them to show themselves to the priests so they could be declared "clean." As they went, the sores that covered their bodies began to disappear.

All but one of the men ran off, received their satisfactory check-up, and disappeared to celebrate their new lease on life. Only one turned around and ran back to Jesus, throwing himself at Christ's feet to thank Him for His mercy. The lepers were physically afflicted. But you and I were once outcasts as well—spiritually lost in a dark and dying world.

My friends, we must never be like the nine men who neglected to give thanks. So take a moment today to show gratitude to God for your salvation and for the spiritual healing that He has provided in the lives of others you love.

What are some similarities between physical leprosy and the effects of sin in your spiritual life?

When is the last time you thanked God for saving you from your sinfulness?

Do you make thanking and praising God a consistent component of your prayer time? Why or why not?

Jesus has reached out to you, just like he reached out to the lepers, and offered to save you from your sinful condition. Have you likewise reached out to your unsaved friends with the hope of the gospel? What would it take for you to do this today?

— *Day Three* —

FINALLY, BRETHREN, WHATEVER THINGS ARE TRUE,
WHATEVER THINGS ARE NOBLE, WHATEVER THINGS ARE
JUST, WHATEVER THINGS ARE PURE, WHATEVER THINGS
ARE LOVELY, WHATEVER THINGS ARE OF GOOD REPORT,
IF THERE IS ANY VIRTUE AND IF THERE IS ANYTHING
PRAISEWORTHY—MEDITATE ON THESE THINGS.

PHILIPPIANS 4:8

In 1948, as my grandfather sat in a hotel room in Modesto, California, he decided to have a conversation with his team. He had recognized the public perception of traveling evangelists and was determined they would protect their integrity as they represented God. That day, he issued a simple assignment to his team: *take an hour to prayerfully consider and catalog the major pitfalls that entrap evangelists and harm their ministry.*

When the group reconvened, their lists were remarkably similar. In short order, they had a series of unofficial guidelines that have become known as the Modesto Manifesto. They would be transparent in their handling of money. They would avoid even the appearance of impropriety by not being alone with anyone who was not their spouse. They would cooperate with any local church who shared their mission to reach the lost. And they would focus on integrity and accuracy in reporting numbers from their campaigns.

While human instinct is to grab as much as we can, elevating ourselves above others, we each have the free will to decide the path we will take. The Bible makes it clear that as citizens of the kingdom of God, we're held to a higher standard—our own "Modesto Manifesto."

How important is integrity to you?

If you were to write your own "manifesto" on integrity, what guidelines would you include?

What is your motivation in exhibiting integrity? Are you driven by a desire to serve and please your heavenly Father? Why or why not?

The question was once asked that if you were put on trial for being a Christian, would there be enough evidence to convict you? Are you living a life of transparent integrity or one weighed down by the sins of this world? Explain.

— *Day Four* —

IF WE CONFESS OUR SINS, HE IS FAITHFUL
AND JUST TO FORGIVE US OUR SINS AND TO
CLEANSE US FROM ALL UNRIGHTEOUSNESS.

1 JOHN 1:9

Night after night, the Australian bus driver stopped to collect a joyful throng of worship-filled riders. He didn't try to hide his disgust and contempt. An alcoholic, his marriage and life were falling apart. He saw no reason for the happiness that his riders expressed.

The year was 1959. The driver, named Ron, was one of many who shuttled attendees back and forth from my grandfather's crusade in Sydney. His irritation would only grow as his passengers sang hymns and praises for what God was doing in their city.

Then, unexpectedly, a miracle took place. Ron's wife was invited to the crusade and surrendered her life to Christ. The following week, at his wife's urging, Ron sat in the same venue to which he had angrily transported many others. At one point, he heard my grandfather call out, "God's speaking to a man here tonight!"

At that moment, Ron heard another voice—one inside him saying "go!" And he went.

God radically transformed Ron's life. He healed him of his addictions. He mended his broken marriage. He even called Ron into ministry. And the couple raised their children in a loving Christian home, building a legacy of faith that remains today.

Ron likely thought he was too far gone to be worthy of Christ's love. In what ways have you felt that same way in your life?

God was bigger than the sin and addiction in Ron's life. Do you recognize a time in your life when the Holy Spirit helped you to walk away from something that ensnared you—or maybe protected you from getting into a bad situation in the first place?

When have you seen a miracle like the one that took place in Ron's life—where a lost soul was radically changed by the incredible love of the Savior? What change did you see in that person?

Ron's wife convinced him to attend the crusade. Subsequently, he and his wife impacted future generations of their family for Christ. How will you shine the "light of life" to your family today?

— *Day Five* —

HE MUST INCREASE, BUT I MUST DECREASE.

JOHN 3:30

Several years ago, the groundbreaking was held for the new Billy Graham Evangelistic Association headquarters in Charlotte, North Carolina. Partway through the ceremony, my grandfather was introduced. Slowed by age, he methodically made his way to the podium as the crowd erupted in enthusiastic applause.

For a moment, he silently stared out at the crowd of admirers. Then he softly uttered the words of John 3:30: "He must increase, but I must decrease." In the middle of a ceremony meant by many to honor him, my grandfather genuinely disregarded—even disdained—the attention and redirected everyone's focus to his Savior, his reason for living.

Our innate motivation is to pump ourselves up, cherish the spotlight, and revel in our successes. Even while we give the glory to God, there's a voice in our heads saying, "Way to go! You did this!" What I find so interesting about my grandfather is that his was a true, ingrained humility. It was a part of who he was as a servant of God.

As you go through your work today, keep these words in mind: "He must increase, but I must decrease." God will use you as you humble yourself and lift Him up.

Is pride a struggle in your life? If so, what steps can you take to turn that over to God?

How would your walk with Christ change if you could truly live out a "John 3:30" life—one in which Jesus increases and you decrease?

What are some areas that God would be able to more greatly use you if you humbled yourself and made yourself available to Him?

As you wrap up this week, take a moment to search your soul. What sins, addictions, attitudes, or doubts are holding you back from growing in your relationship with Jesus? Take some time to pray, confessing your sins and laying your burdens at the feet of Christ.

SESSION
Three

A NEW HEART
AND PURPOSE

---∞---

YOU WILL NEVER UNDERSTAND
WHO YOU ARE UNTIL YOU
UNDERSTAND WHO GOD IS.
BILLY GRAHAM

---∞---

WELCOME

You may not know it by looking at me, but I love working on cars. I enjoy restoring old vehicles that are long past their prime and turning them into well-oiled, smooth-running machines. My current project is a yellow 1985 K-Series Chevrolet pickup truck.

But a funny thing happens from time to time when you are working on cars. You install a new component, and—for some reason—there's a part or two left over. Maybe it's a screw or a spring or even a little piece of plastic. You uninstall and reinstall the component, rifle through the instructions, and even search the internet, but the piece just doesn't seem to have a reason for existing. It doesn't have a purpose.

Not being able to discover the purpose of the random automotive piece is frustrating. But it pales in comparison to a struggle that many people have on a daily basis. Around the world, people struggle with the question of their own path and purpose. They wander aimlessly through life, going from one job, one relationship, and one momentary pleasure to the next, never truly understanding who they are or what they're on this earth to accomplish.

I recently read the account of a star athlete who, after winning the championship and being named MVP, sat on the team bus, frustrated by the question of purpose. He was in his twenties and had already reached the pinnacle of his profession. He was famous, rich, and successful. Was that all there was? What was he missing? What was his purpose?

Finding your purpose is a universal challenge that is shared by all of mankind. Whether a person lives in squalor or is the CEO of a Fortune 500 company, that nagging voice demanding a purpose for being does not discriminate.

So, how do you find and stay on the path that has been laid out for you as a child of God? How do you avoid the pitfalls of a world that seeks to lead you astray and keep your focus in the right place? Moreover, what is your purpose during your days on this earth?

In today's session, we're going to see what the Bible has to say about purpose and about surrendering everything you have—your past, your present, and your future—into your Master's hand.

SHARE

Begin your group time by inviting anyone to share his or her insights from last week's personal study. As you begin this week's study, discuss one of the following questions:

- Have you ever taken a wrong turn and gotten lost? How did it feel as you were blindly searching for the right path?

– *or* –

- What comes to mind when you think about your "purpose" in life?

READ

Invite someone to read aloud the following passage. Listen for fresh insights as you hear the verses being read, and then discuss the questions that follow.

> *For I know the thoughts that I think toward you, says the LORD, thoughts of peace and not of evil, to give you a future and a hope. Then you will call upon Me and go and pray to Me, and I will listen to you. And you will seek Me and find Me, when you search for Me with all your heart (Jeremiah 29:11–13).*

God says that He has a plan for each of us, including "a future and a hope." How does it feel to know this?

Many people focus on Jeremiah 29:11 without reading verses 12–13. What does prayer and calling on God have to do with finding His plan for your life?

Do you search for God "with all your heart" each day? If so, what does that look like?

WATCH

Play the video for session three. As you and your group watch, use the following outline to record any thoughts or key points that stand out to you.

NOTES

We try to find our purpose in work, relationships, or vices. We chase empty dreams and broken promises. We often go our own way and miss our purpose.

Like a compass, we need to have Jesus as our fixed point and keep our eyes on Him.

This world offers many things to pull us onto the wrong path. Maybe it's a relationship that we know isn't right. Maybe it's an addiction, sin, or passion that has become an idol.

We go down the wrong path because we refuse to listen to guidance that is offered. The Bible speaks to every aspect of our lives and gives us that guidance. There isn't an issue in the world that isn't addressed in some way by the Bible. How often, though, do we stop to listen?

Going our own way will only lead to confusion and despair. We can't be so sure of our own experience and expertise that we fail to stop and see what God's Word has to say.

Our mission grows out of our purpose, which is to have a relationship with Jesus and worship Him with all that we are.

My grandfather, Billy Graham, found his purpose when he fell to his knees and surrendered everything into his Master's hand. From that day forward, God used him in extraordinary ways. He will do the same for us.

DISCUSS

Spend a few minutes as a group discussing what you just watched and exploring these concepts together.

1. I accepted Christ as a child but fully surrendered my past, present, and future to Him as a teenager. Can you recall a time when you fully gave everything over to Jesus? How did that change your path and purpose?

2. Where do you tend to find your happiness and joy—work, family, volunteering, or even watching sports or political debates? How is that gratification different from knowing your path and purpose in Jesus?

3. Being honest, do you find it easy to keep your compass pointed to Jesus, or does the world pull you in different directions so that you lose focus?

4. God says in Jeremiah 29:11 that He has a plan for your life. In Proverbs 3:6, He says that He will direct your path. Can you say that is true in your life? Why and/or how?

5. When you're faced with a struggle or question, where do you tend to go for answers? Would you agree that—even millennia later—the Bible is a living book that still offers guidance for every issue you may encounter today? Why or why not?

6. Having watched the analogy of the pen and paper, would you personally say that you are in the Master's hand, fully understanding and embracing your purpose as a child of the King? Why or why not?

PRAY

As a child of your heavenly Father, you have access to Him directly through prayer. So close today's session by taking a few minutes to seek Him and His guidance in your life. Here are a few ideas of what you could pray about based on what you learned in this session:

- Ask forgiveness for the times when you have gone your own way rather than seeking God's path and guidance.
- Prayerfully surrender your past, present, and future to God's will.
- Commit to focusing your "compass" on Jesus, with heaven as your destination.
- Seek God with all of your heart, knowing that—when you do—He will meet you where you are.
- Thank God for His faithfulness and for having a plan for your life as you live for Him.

RESPOND

In a perfect world, a compass always points north and allows the user to set a bearing so he or she can follow the right path. However, magnetic deviations can cause errors with the compass, which skews the direction. While I'm sure that most of you would say that your spiritual compass is pointing toward Christ, I would encourage you to consider if there are any "deviations" that may be pulling you off course. These may not be bad things in and of themselves, but they still may be taking the place of Christ in your life and could require a correction of sorts. In the space below, write a short list of issues that are distracting you from your walk with Jesus and how you can fix your compass back onto Him.

1. _____   Fix: _____
2. _____   Fix: _____
3. _____   Fix: _____

Between-Sessions
PERSONAL STUDY

---⬦---

*R*eflect on the material you've covered this week by engaging in the following between-sessions activities. Each day offers a short reading adapted from my devotional book *Redeemed*, along with a few questions for you to ponder. If you find it helpful, I encourage you to write down your thoughts. At the start of the next session, feel free to share any insights you learned with the group. Remember, however, the primary goal for this section is your own spiritual growth.

— *Day One* —

YOU DID NOT CHOOSE ME, BUT I CHOSE YOU
AND APPOINTED YOU THAT YOU SHOULD GO
AND BEAR FRUIT, AND THAT YOUR FRUIT
SHOULD REMAIN, THAT WHATEVER YOU ASK
THE FATHER IN MY NAME HE MAY GIVE YOU.

JOHN 15:16

This is going to be fun, I thought as the teacher instructed my third-grade class to draw a picture of what we wanted to be when we grew up. I glanced around the room and quickly saw that most of the other boys wanted to be football players. I'm a fan of the sport as well, but I found myself tracing out a David Clark aviation headset and an open Bible.

Simply put, I wanted to do what my dad did. I wanted to fly around the world and tell people about Jesus. From an early point in my life, I was already sensing God's calling and direction, pointing me toward a life in ministry.

My friends, just as God called me into ministry, He has called you as well. Perhaps your mission field is the public school where you teach, the hospital where you serve, or the office where you work. Maybe your ministry is to your clients or your employees.

Paul tells us in Romans 12 that we are different parts of the same body, and we've each been equipped for different work. The key component is that God is the One who gives us the calling—and He has prepared us uniquely for it.

What have you sensed God calling you to do? Where has He led you to serve?

How has God prepared you for your calling?

What may be holding you back from pursuing your calling from God? What can you do to fully embrace it?

If your calling—the ministry God has for you—isn't clear to you at this point, how will you prayerfully ask Him to reveal it to you?

— *Day Two* —

DO NOT LAY UP FOR YOURSELVES
TREASURES ON EARTH, WHERE MOTH AND
RUST DESTROY AND WHERE THIEVES BREAK
IN AND STEAL; BUT LAY UP FOR YOURSELVES
TREASURES IN HEAVEN, WHERE NEITHER
MOTH NOR RUST DESTROYS AND WHERE
THIEVES DO NOT BREAK IN AND STEAL.

MATTHEW 6:19–20

Several years ago, my friend Rodney and I were driving on Parramatta Road in Sydney, which is lined with luxury car dealerships on either side. My eyes caught every color and shape as we made our way down the street—Maseratis, Lamborghinis, Porsches, and more. I pointed them out, saying, "Man, I'd love to have that car," or, "Would you look at that one?"

As I was transfixed by the automobiles, I heard Rodney say, "Wow, I would love to be over there!" I turned to see which car he was checking out and was immediately convicted. Rodney wasn't pointing out a bright red sports car. He was looking at a park full of teenagers who were leaning on BMX bikes and rolling on skateboards. While I was looking at cars, his mind was focused on sharing the hope of Christ with young people he had never met, souls who were likely crying out for the hope found in Jesus Christ.

My friends, whatever you're dealing with today, try to be like Rodney. Turn your focus away from the material things and concentrate on what is important in the scope of eternity. Seek time with your Savior, in prayer and study, and allow Him to reorder your priorities.

What worldly pleasures are distracting you from following Christ with all of your heart?

What is one concrete way you can reorder your priorities to put Christ at the center of your life?

Rodney's heart broke for the lost people around him. Could the same be said for you as you go through your days? Why or why not?

What are some practical ways you can begin to have a more eternally focused (as opposed to materially focused) mindset?

— *Day Three* —

IF ANY OF YOU LACKS WISDOM, LET HIM ASK
OF GOD, WHO GIVES TO ALL LIBERALLY AND
WITHOUT REPROACH, AND IT WILL BE GIVEN
TO HIM. BUT LET HIM ASK IN FAITH, WITH NO
DOUBTING, FOR HE WHO DOUBTS IS LIKE A WAVE
OF THE SEA DRIVEN AND TOSSED BY THE WIND.

JAMES 1:5–6

My grandfather's 1949 crusade in Los Angeles was a watershed moment for his ministry. It made him a household name and launched decades of evangelism around the world. At the time, however, it was a struggle. The crusade was scheduled to last three weeks, and at the end of that time the team debated extending the campaign.

That's when Stuart Hamblen, a radio personality, invited my grandfather on to his show and announced he would attend the crusade. Ultimately, Hamblen accepted Christ in a tear-filled moment of repentance. My grandfather knew they had to continue. There were other "Stuart Hamblens" out there who needed to hear the Good News of Christ's love.

It was soon evident God was moving in their midst. But by the end of the fifth week they were facing the same question: continue or conclude? At the same time, a massive storm was brewing and on track for downtown Los Angeles. My grandfather and his team prayed for guidance. Much to the surprise of the meteorologists, the storm veered away!

The Los Angeles crusade lasted eight weeks, with some 3,000 people placing their trust in Christ. What began as a semi-successful outreach blossomed into something so much greater as my grandfather sought God and followed His guiding hand.

What struggles are you facing today? How are you seeking God's guidance in response to those struggles?

How might God offer you guidance as you seek Him? (Maybe through the biblical advice of a friend or counselor, through a moment of encouragement, or through a verse of Scripture?)

When you receive the guidance you are seeking, will you accept it, or might you be tempted to ignore it because you have your own goals or agenda? Explain.

My grandfather's response to the guidance he received resulted in many people accepting the eternal hope of Christ. How might God work through you as you follow His guidance?

— *Day Four* —

> BUT INDEED FOR THIS PURPOSE I HAVE
> RAISED YOU UP, THAT I MAY SHOW MY
> POWER IN YOU, AND THAT MY NAME
> MAY BE DECLARED IN ALL THE EARTH.
>
> EXODUS 9:16

In 2006, I was the pastor of a growing church in Raleigh, North Carolina. God had brought me to this place, and I had no desire to go anywhere else. But one day, I was mowing the lawn when God said, "It's time." He was calling me to serve at the Billy Graham Evangelistic Association.

I was in turmoil and wrestled with this calling. As the tears flowed, the phone rang. At the other end was an evangelist from Texas whom my father met while they were ministering in Central America. "Will," he said, "God laid it on my heart to call you. I know you're in the middle of making a big decision right now, and I want to pray with you . . ." God further confirmed His calling with Scripture that He laid on my heart.

Perhaps you have found yourself in a similar situation where you knew God was calling you to take a leap, but you were too afraid or too comfortable to move. When God shows you His will, you must prayerfully listen and obey. Because I followed His leading into evangelism, I've had the incredible blessing of watching people around the world find their eternal hope in Jesus.

God has a purpose for your life too. It may not be easy, but it's worth it!

Has God ever told you, "It's time"? If so, did you follow His lead-ing? Or did something hold you back? Explain.

Do you ever struggle with comfortability? How often have you chosen to stay comfortable rather than stretching yourself by following God's leading?

In my situation, God spoke to me and then reaffirmed the direc-tion through a call from a trusted friend and through Scripture. How has he spoken to you or guided you?

If God were to speak to you today, would you be prepared to obey? Why or why not?

— *Day Five* —

YOUR EARS SHALL HEAR A WORD
BEHIND YOU, SAYING, "THIS IS THE
WAY, WALK IN IT," WHENEVER YOU
TURN TO THE RIGHT HAND OR
WHENEVER YOU TURN TO THE LEFT.

ISAIAH 30:21

Just after the crusade in Los Angeles launched my grandfather into national prominence, he found himself at a luncheon with some of the heaviest hitters in Hollywood, including Frank Freeman, the president of Paramount Pictures. During the conversation, Mr. Freeman asked my grandfather to consider acting in one of their films.

I'm sure my grandfather was flattered by the offer, but he quickly declined. In front of the "who's who" of Tinseltown, my grandfather shared that he had been called to preach the gospel and would never do anything else. Later, in 1964, a handful of folks encouraged my grandfather to run for president. He hastily ended that conversation as well. He categorically refused to run for office, declaring yet again that he was called to preach.

Billy Graham was not an actor. He was not a politician. He was an evangelist!

We often talk about God opening doors, but just because a door is open doesn't mean it's a gift from Him. Instead, it could be a temptation trying to steer us away from our calling. So, when you see a door opening, be ready to move *or* stay. Most important, seek God through reading the Bible and through prayer so you know which action to take.

Do you sense that God is opening a door for you to go through right now? If so, how is God's Word confirming that decision?

As you consider the open doors in your life, what role does your faith play in helping you decide the right path?

Have you ever hastily gone through an open door only to realize that it was a mistake? If so, what was the result of your action?

Have you committed to spend time each day in prayer and Bible study? If so, how has that helped you discern God's plan for your life?

SESSION
Four

A New Outlook on Difficulties

———∞———

THE BIBLE TEACHES US THAT WE ARE
TO BE PATIENT IN SUFFERING. TEARS
BECOME TELESCOPES TO HEAVEN,
BRINGING ETERNITY A LITTLE CLOSER.
BILLY GRAHAM

———∞———

WELCOME

Regardless of when you're going through this study, I can guarantee you one thing: When you look at the world around you, difficulties abound.

It might be hurricanes, tornadoes, wildfires, and earthquakes. It could be wars, mass shootings, or political turmoil. Closer to home, you or a loved one may be dealing with sudden loss, divorce, financial stress, or a life-threatening disease. You could be embroiled in relationship issues within your family, your work, or your church. You very well may be sick and tired . . . and tired of being sick and tired.

My friends, we live in a broken and fallen world. One day, as we continue to follow Jesus, we will know the beauty and perfection of heaven. But in the meantime, suffering is a certainty.

Of course, pain of this type often leads to the "why" questions. *Why does God allow good people to suffer? Why does God not answer when I beg for His help? Why am I going through this when others are not?*

I don't have any good answers for you. The mystery of suffering is as old as mankind itself. Not one person who has ever walked this earth—including Jesus—has fully avoided heartache and pain.

I wish that I could tell you that being a follower of Christ gives you a free pass and somehow protects you from the trials of this world. Unfortunately, that's not the case. In fact, Jesus told us in John 16:33 that the opposite is true:

*"These things I have spoken to you, that in Me you may
have peace. In the world you will have tribulation; but be
of good cheer, I have overcome the world."*

Yes, there will be hard times. It's guaranteed. But there's also
a promise: Christ has overcome the world, and He is in control!

Today, we're going to discuss how we can have a new outlook on difficulties, and how God is in our midst as we make
our way through this troubled world.

SHARE

Begin your group time by inviting anyone to share his or her
insights from last week's personal study. As you begin this
week's study, discuss one of the following questions:

- What difficult issues—locally, nationally, or
  internationally—are in the news this week? How might
  God be at work in these situations?

– or –

- Do you find it's easier to draw close to God when you're
  on the mountaintop (the good times) or in the valleys
  (times of trial)? Why?

READ

Invite someone to read aloud the following passage. Listen for fresh insights as you hear the verses being read, and then discuss the questions that follow.

> *My brethren, count it all joy when you fall into various trials, knowing that the testing of your faith produces patience. But let patience have its perfect work, that you may be perfect and complete, lacking nothing (James 1:2–4).*

How easy is it to "count it all joy" when you are going through a difficult, life-altering struggle?

In what ways might God use trials to develop your relationship with Him?

What do you think James means when he says "let patience have its perfect work" so you may be complete?

WATCH

Play the video for session four. As you and your group watch, use the following outline to record any thoughts or key points that stand out to you.

NOTES

Our calling as children of God gives us an eternal perspective, but it's still difficult to jump the roadblocks that stand in our way.

When hardships come, we aren't to get frustrated or quit. We shouldn't consider it to be a closed door. We're to see that God is working in and through the adversity to strengthen our faith and mold us to serve Him better.

There are a few things that we are *not* told in the Bible. We are *not* told that if we endure, it will get easier. We also are *not* told that by tackling adversity we will be guaranteed success.

In spite of all this, there will be joy and patience and perfection as we serve God in the midst of hardships.

We need to have faith that God is at work and has a plan for us—even if the pain is too great for us to see it at the moment.

Know that as followers of Christ, our trials are temporary. The best days—the hope of Jesus—remain in front of us.

Spending time in the presence of God through prayer and Bible reading is key for growing in our faith and learning to trust the Lord during times of difficulty.

While it may be easier to walk away, we need to allow God to use our struggles to refine us and use it for His glory.

DISCUSS

Spend a few minutes as a group discussing what you just watched and exploring these concepts together.

1. In your group, there are likely many difficulties that each member is facing. Some you may know about, while others are confidential. If you are open to sharing, what specific issues are you facing today?

2. As you endure struggles and hardships, are you able to see God at work? Whether your answer is yes or no, how does that make you feel?

3. How likely are you to view difficulties as a closed door—a reason to get frustrated or quit? What's your motivation to keep going?

4. Is it even possible to "count it all joy" as you are going through a difficult time? How?

5. How does your faith impact your response to suffering? How likely are you to have an eternal focus when faced with trials and troubles?

6. We often try to put on a strong or happy face and hide our pain from others. How likely are you to share your struggles with a close Christian friend or counselor? What are the advantages to doing so?

PRAY

Difficulties are universal. We all have them. Thankfully, we also serve a God who wants to bring us His peace that passes all understanding as we draw near to Him. Take a few minutes to pray, laying your burdens at His feet. Here are a few ideas of what you could pray about based on what you learned in this session:

- Acknowledge your struggles, turning those difficult situations over to God.
- Pray for God's peace, hope, and comfort in the darkness of your struggles.
- Ask for strength and courage to push forward in the midst of pain or adversity, for God's glory.
- Thank Jesus for being your rock in the storms of life and for the promise that when the temporary suffering of this world is over, you will be able to spend eternity in His presence.
- Pray for one another, recognizing that we all have spoken or unspoken prayer requests and needs.

RESPOND

My guess is that most of you are going through something difficult right now. If you aren't, just wait. It won't be long before you too are faced with a struggle that will seem insurmountable in your own power. As followers of Christ, however, we have an eternal perspective that is much different from the world's. We have the hope that the temporary struggles of this broken realm pale in comparison to the glory that awaits us. Further, we know that we serve a heavenly Father who loves us, comforts us, and is at work in the midst of our pain. In the space below, prayerfully write a short letter to God, expressing your hurts and struggles. As you read in 1 Peter 5:7, you can cast your cares on Him, because He cares for you!

Between-Sessions
PERSONAL STUDY

⎯⎯∞⎯⎯

*T*he mystery of suffering is perhaps one of the most difficult issues to work through. We all want life to be carefree and easy, but we live in a fallen world. Thankfully, we can find comfort in our Savior. This week, as you read through the following excerpts adapted from *Redeemed*, I pray that God will encourage you in the midst of your struggles as you focus on Him. As before, I encourage you to write down your thoughts. At the start of the next session, feel free to share any insights you learned with the group. Remember, however, the primary goal for this section is your own spiritual growth.

— *Day One* —

AND THE LORD, HE IS THE ONE WHO
GOES BEFORE YOU. HE WILL BE WITH YOU,
HE WILL NOT LEAVE YOU NOR FORSAKE
YOU; DO NOT FEAR NOR BE DISMAYED.
DEUTERONOMY 31:8

It was December 2008, and I was about to preach in Thiruvalla. This city, located in southwest India, is one of the safest in the country for Christians. I was there with the blessing of the government to hold an evangelistic outreach. But there was a problem. Elections were scheduled for the next day, and a group was holding a rally for their candidates.

Regardless, our evangelistic campaign was about to start. So we climbed into the car and edged out onto the roadway. Within moments, our vehicle was engulfed by the mass of people that had filled the street. Countless hands began rocking the car back and forth.

In that moment, I was the most scared I've ever been on one of my international journeys. I was surrounded by a mob, and there was no way out. But as we cried out to God, the disposition of the crowd began to change. Instead of latching on, they moved like a river around us.

I'm still not sure if it was the crowd that changed or if it was our level of peace as we called on the Lord. Either way, we were able to move again, and God provided a wonderful harvest as we proclaimed His name.

When was a time in your life that you were afraid? Did you call on God in your moment of need? If so, what was His response?

The diagnosis of cancer, the dissolution of a family, the death of a loved one, the loss of a job . . . all can make you feel like you're trapped in a situation where you're being threatened and there's no way out. How do you respond when faced with a difficulty like this?

God was with us in that car, and He's with you right now, whatever you're facing. How easy or difficult is it to cling to that promise? Why?

My perspective changed in that car as we called on God for protection and peace. How have you found that God changes your perspective as well—regardless of your difficult situation—when you spend time with Him?

— *Day Two* —

FOR WHAT IS YOUR LIFE? IT IS EVEN
A VAPOR THAT APPEARS FOR A LITTLE
TIME AND THEN VANISHES AWAY.

JAMES 4:14

Time. It's the greatest resource you have. With every new day you have less of it than you did the day before. You can't save any today to spend tomorrow. You can't grip it so tightly that it will not slip away. You can only use it when you have it.

The Bible tells us that our time on earth is short. As James describes it, we are like "a vapor that appears for a little time and then vanishes away." Since our time is limited, we need to be aware of how we are using it to impact a dark world with the light of Jesus. Paul writes, "See then that you walk circumspectly, not as fools but as wise, redeeming the time, because the days are evil" (Ephesians 5:15–16). Just as we are accountable for wisely using the gifts we are given, we are accountable for how we use our time for the kingdom of God.

My grandfather said one of the greatest surprises of his life was the "brevity" of it. He used every moment well, yet was amazed at how quickly it slipped away. My friends, today is a gift, and tomorrow isn't guaranteed. So, for the sake of your family, your Savior, and your eternity, use your time wisely.

How would you say that you have used the time you've been given by God?

We live in a temporary world, where even suffering and trauma will eventually give way to eternity. In light of this, how important is the hope you have in Christ?

It's important to make the most of the limited time you have on this earth. How can you better help and serve those around you who are hurting?

If you are a "vapor," here today and gone tomorrow, what are a few things you can do to make an eternal impact on those around you (your friends, family, coworkers, community)?

— *Day Three* —

So David went to Baal Perazim,
and David defeated them there;
and he said, "The Lord has broken
through my enemies before me,
like a breakthrough of water."

2 SAMUEL 5:20

David was the freshly anointed king of Israel. He had just taken Jerusalem. He was happy, and his people were excited. Life was good. But as soon as his enemy, the Philistines, heard that he had been named king, they moved swiftly to take him out. David went from the highest of highs to the lowest of lows. His very life was suddenly at risk.

David responded by inquiring of the Lord, which should be our initial step as well when faced with a difficult situation. Now, while there are no guarantees on *when* God will answer, know that He *will* answer. In David's case, God answered immediately, which brings us to his second step. He obediently followed God's leading by marching into battle.

As a result, God led the Israelites in such a rousing victory that David proclaimed, "The Lord has broken through my enemies before me, like a breakthrough of water" (2 Samuel 5:20). My friends, if life is going good, now is the time to be preparing yourself spiritually for the coming battle. And if you are already going through a crisis, know that Jesus is with you.

As He did for David, God can bring about a breakthrough in your life.

Describe a time in your life when you went from the highest of highs to the lowest of lows.

 What tends to be your initial reaction when faced with a trial or crisis? Is it to inquire of the Lord as David did? Why or why not?

 When God answered David's prayer, he responded immediately by following God's orders. Do you think you would have done the same? Why or why not?

 Would you say that you are spiritually prepared for the inevitable difficulties of life? Explain.

— *Day Four* —

HOW BEAUTIFUL UPON THE MOUNTAINS
ARE THE FEET OF HIM WHO BRINGS GOOD
NEWS, WHO PROCLAIMS PEACE, WHO
BRINGS GLAD TIDINGS OF GOOD THINGS,
WHO PROCLAIMS SALVATION, WHO
SAYS TO ZION, "YOUR GOD REIGNS!"

ISAIAH 52:7

My grandparents sat down to visit with a man from Botswana. He was one of thousands of evangelists taking part in my grandfather's Amsterdam '86 gathering. Based on his clothing, they could tell he came from humble means. Even so, happiness was ever-present on his face.

The man said there were few Christians in his country and his labor was not always fruitful. He persevered, however, because it was his calling from God. As the discussion continued, it came out that he was educated at Cambridge University— one of the most prestigious institutes in the world! He likely could have done anything he chose. But instead, he was living a difficult and dangerous life for the sake of the gospel.

Have you ever considered the cost of following Jesus? For some, the cost is social. For others, it is financial. For some, there is a real physical cost to be paid. In the case of the evangelist from Botswana, it's safe to assume his was a combination of all three. But he was blessed! He paid the price as an ambassador of God and exhibited a peace many long to find.

My friends, there is a cost to following Jesus. But in the scope of eternity, it is worth it!

Have you ever had to pay a social, financial, or physical price for following Christ? If so, how did you find the price to be worth it?

If you were in a difficult situation and had to take a stand for Jesus today, how would you react?

The evangelist from Botswana had peace, even as he was dealing with many hardships. How do you find peace when dealing with difficulties in your life?

How does the hope of eternity with Christ help to make your present struggles easier to bear?

— *Day Five* —

BUT AS IT IS WRITTEN: "EYE HAS NOT
SEEN, NOR EAR HEARD, NOR HAVE
ENTERED INTO THE HEART OF MAN THE
THINGS WHICH GOD HAS PREPARED
FOR THOSE WHO LOVE HIM."
1 CORINTHIANS 2:9

My grandfather was one of the most heaven-focused people I've ever met. Long before he slipped into eternity on February 21, 2018, he made the following proclamation: "One day you're going to hear that Billy Graham has died. But don't believe it! For on that day I will be more alive than ever before. I will have just changed addresses!"

I believe heaven became increasingly real to him as he aged into his nineties. In many ways, this world was no longer his home. Likewise, you may be clinging to the hope of heaven as your anchor. Perhaps you are dealing with a terminal disease, or you have lost a loved one recently. If so, I pray you're finding the peace of God as you walk this valley.

I would also encourage you to cling to the *reality* of heaven. Heaven is a *real* place where you will reside for eternity with your Savior. It's not just a different address . . . in heaven, there will be no mourning, pain, hunger, or thirst. There will be a place specially prepared for you. The old will be gone, and all things will be made new!

So, if you've surrendered your life to Jesus, don't fear death. Instead, anxiously anticipate heaven!

What images come to mind when you think of heaven?

Is heaven a hope or a reality for you? Why?

My grandfather wasn't afraid of death. In some ways, he longed to pass from this world into heaven. Can you say the same? Why or why not?

In what ways do you believe that heaven will be far better than earth?

SESSION
Five

A NEW LONGING TO SHARE CHRIST

THE SPIRIT GOES AHEAD OF US WHEN WE
WITNESS—PREPARING THE WAY, GIVING US
THE WORDS, AND GRANTING US COURAGE.
BILLY GRAHAM

WELCOME

People will often give me a somewhat shocked look when I say that I see miracles all the time. Perhaps they expect me to follow with stories about witnessing the lame walk or the afflicted made well. But that's not what I'm talking about. While many pray and dream of physical healing, the true miracle comes when people are made spiritually whole.

Every time I offer an invitation to begin a relationship with Jesus Christ, and people accept that hope and surrender their lives to Him, I see those who were once dead brought to life. I see the miracle of broken, hurting individuals finding peace and rest. I watch as tears stream down the faces of longing souls who finally understand they can be forgiven and spend eternity with Jesus—not because of anything they can do but because Christ's sacrifice has made a way.

All around us are people who are trying to do more good than bad . . . somehow hoping the scales will tip in their favor and they'll be able to earn a path to heaven. Others believe they are destined for an eternity in hell and there's nothing they can do to change that fact.

If we open our eyes, we'll see people who are hurting and desperately in need of love and hope. And guess what? We have the answer! God has opened our eyes to the promise of glory as the truth of the gospel has been revealed to us.

Now, let me ask you this. If people are hurting and searching for forgiveness and peace, and if you have the answer they're seeking, what are you doing about it? Are you sharing the light that you've found so that others may have it as well? Or are you hiding it under the proverbial bushel (see Matthew 5:15), too afraid or shy to pass it on to others?

My friends, the last several sessions have been leading up to this. We know that Christ can give us love, freedom, purpose, and a new outlook, and now it's time to burst out the doors of the church and proclaim that incredible hope to others.

Eternity is at stake!

SHARE

Begin your group time by inviting anyone to share his or her insights from last week's personal study. As you begin this week's study, discuss one of the following questions:

- Have you ever led somebody to Christ? If so, how would you describe the experience of seeing "new life" begin in a person who was without hope?

– *or* –

- Have you ever seen a miracle take place? If so, what was it?

READ

Invite someone to read aloud the following passage. Listen for fresh insights as you hear the verses being read, and then discuss the questions that follow.

> *Then Jesus went about all the cities and villages, teaching in their synagogues, preaching the gospel of the kingdom, and healing every sickness and every disease among the people. But when He saw the multitudes, He was moved with compassion for them, because they were weary and scattered, like sheep having no shepherd. Then He said to His disciples, "The harvest truly is plentiful, but the laborers are few. Therefore pray the Lord of the harvest to send out laborers into His harvest" (Matthew 9:35–38).*

Matthew describes the people as "weary and scattered, like sheep having no shepherd." How would you describe the people with whom you interact on a daily basis?

Jesus was moved with compassion for the people. His heart hurt as He watched them struggling through life. What is your reaction when you see longing souls who are wandering away from the Savior?

When you consider the world around you (and, in particular, your sphere of influence), would you say that the harvest is plentiful? Explain.

WATCH

Play the video for session five. As you and your group watch, use the following outline to record any thoughts or key points that stand out to you.

NOTES

The very first Bible verse I memorized as a young boy remains one of my favorites: "For the Holy Spirit will teach you in that very hour what you ought to say" (Luke 12:12). And it's 100 percent true.

If we are truly focused on Jesus—on the change He made in our lives and the eternal needs of those around us—Christ will continually show us people who need Him and opportunities to share the hope that is within us.

Recognize that people are hungry for the hope of Jesus. We can't underestimate the hopelessness of this world and the desire within those around us for the peace and hope that we have.

Be discerning in sensing opportunities that God is providing. How often do we watch as people struggle through life without sharing with them that they can have true hope for eternity?

When opportunities do arise, we must be forthright in sharing the love of Christ. We could come up with a million excuses not to step out in faith and share the love and peace we've found, but let's not miss those openings that God provides.

I pray that we will have an urgency in our spirits to share Him with others and that He would allow us to see the miracle of people finding true freedom in Christ.

Understand that God is at work in every situation. By being faithful and obedient, God can and will use us for His glory!

Take heart in knowing that sharing the gospel isn't about us. It's about lifting high the name of Jesus and allowing Him to work in other people's lives.

DISCUSS

Spend a few minutes as a group discussing what you just watched and exploring these concepts together.

1. What does your relationship with Christ mean to you? Why is it important to "let your light shine" and pass on what you have discovered about Jesus to others?

2. As you consider your own situation, where are some places that you could offer the hope of Christ to those around you (at work, at the store, at school)?

3. Do you agree that people are hungry for the hope of Jesus? Speaking candidly, what are some of the reasons you may *not* choose to share your faith with others?

4. As I mentioned in today's session, both Todd and I were led to offer the hope of Jesus to strangers, but we had very different results. Talk about a time when the Holy Spirit nudged you to witness to somebody. How did you respond? What was the outcome?

5. Have you ever asked God to open your eyes to the spiritual needs of those around you? If so, share that experience. If not, will you commit to praying for opportunities to shine the light of Jesus? Why or why not?

6. You've heard me say that when it comes to sharing about Jesus, eternity is at stake. What does that mean? Do you ever think about eternity—both heaven and hell—when considering the "weary and scattered" around you?

PRAY

My friends, in this session we've been talking about the difference between hope and despair, between peace and turmoil, and heaven and hell. We've been given the cure for this broken and sin-sick world, and we have the opportunity to pass it along to others. Ponder this as you close your time together in prayer. Here are a few ideas of what to pray about based on everything we've discussed in this session:

- Seek forgiveness if there were times when you ignored the Holy Spirit's prompting to share your faith.
- Commit to sharing the love of Jesus with others and ask for "open eyes" to see the spiritual needs of those around you.
- Pray for courage to step out and boldly grab the opportunities you are given by the Holy Spirit.
- Humbly request comfort and confidence for the times when the message is not received well by others, understanding that they aren't rejecting you.

• Ask for God's favor and that you will be able to see the "fruit of the harvest" as you proclaim His name to others.

RESPOND

The apostle Paul says that "faith comes by hearing, and hearing by the word of God" (Romans 10:17). It's vitally important to live your life in a way that points others to Christ, but eventually you need to open your mouth and speak. Where do you begin? One idea is to start with your testimony—your story of how God changed your life. Share about the person you were before He came into your life and the hope you have now. It's your story, so it will be easy to remember, and people can't really argue with your personal experiences. Take a few minutes to write down some notes about your testimony, using more paper if needed. Then, prayerfully, be ready to share when the Holy Spirit opens the door!

Final

PERSONAL STUDY

———◇◇◇———

As we close this study, I pray that you have been encouraged in your faith and challenged to step out and share Christ with the world around you. This week, read through the following excerpts adapted from *Redeemed,* and again write down your thoughts in response to the questions. Also, be responsive to the leading of the Holy Spirit as your eyes are opened to the eternal needs of your friends, neighbors, or coworkers. Be sure to share with your group leader or group members in the upcoming weeks any key points or insights that stood out to you.

— *Day One* —

REJOICE ALWAYS, PRAY WITHOUT CEASING, IN
EVERYTHING GIVE THANKS; FOR THIS IS THE
WILL OF GOD IN CHRIST JESUS FOR YOU.
1 THESSALONIANS 5:16-18

"Pray, pray, pray," my grandfather said as we sat in front of the fireplace in the log home he and my grandmother had built from the ground up in the 1950s. "Study, study, study. Looking back, I wish I had done so much more of both."

I had come to seek his advice after deciding to serve with the Billy Graham Evangelistic Association. I'll admit his response left me pondering. Nearly every time I visited, he was either praying or reading God's Word. How could it be that he felt inadequate in these areas?

Perhaps sensing my question, he explained, "I wish I knew the Bible as well as your grandmother. She knows it better than anyone I have ever met. And we could have done so much more if we had taken fewer speaking engagements and spent more time on our knees."

You don't have to be an evangelist to gain eternal value from spending time in prayer and study. Rather, you will be blessed beyond measure as you develop your relationship with God in this way. Further, it is wise to be careful about doing "too much." Even if what you are doing is noble, you can't let it get in the way of what is most important in the scope of eternity.

My friends, take heed of the lesson my grandfather learned and passed along to me. Make prayer and studying the Bible a priority in your life.

Why do you think my grandfather felt that he could have done even more for the kingdom of God if he had taken fewer speaking engagements?

Are you "too busy" to spend significant time in the Bible and in prayer? If so, what practical steps could you take to prioritize your time with Jesus?

How do you tend to feel as you delve into God's Word and presence?

In what ways would you be a better witness to your friends and family if you invested more time in drawing close to Jesus?

— *Day Two* —

LET YOUR LIGHT SO SHINE BEFORE MEN,
THAT THEY MAY SEE YOUR GOOD WORKS
AND GLORIFY YOUR FATHER IN HEAVEN.

MATTHEW 5:16

A few years back, we held an evangelistic outreach in Las Piedras, Uruguay. The city had been in the process of building a soccer stadium but midway through had run out of funds. Stretching into the sky, you could see the towering walls and skeleton of the stadium. But inside, the façade were merely the brackets of would-be seating, unfinished and without benches.

Even incomplete, this would be the host arena for our evangelistic event. The local Christians decided the best way to impact their community for the gospel was to help improve the stadium—and do so in a manner that exhibited not half-heartedness but excellence. So they painted the concrete walls, the railings, and everything else that needed a fresh coating. They also purchased stadium lighting. This would remain as a gift from the Christians of Las Piedras to the rest of the community, allowing the soccer teams to finally play night games.

When we arrived, the stadium sparkled with a newfound vibrancy. The mayor was so impressed he said the local church would always have a place at his table. It was his desire that the churches hear the needs of the city and have an opportunity to be a part of the solution!

What is one thing you can do today to take the step from "ordinary" to "excellent" in the way you serve others in your community?

The Christians in Las Piedras showed Christ's love through service and generosity to others. What are some ways you can do that today?

When the believers exemplified the love of Jesus, people took notice (right up to the mayor's office). Are people watching how you live? If so, what are they seeing?

The Christians of Las Piedras worked hard to provide for their neighbors—and there likely came a point when they were asked why they were serving others in this way. If you had been a part of this group, how would you have responded to this open door to share the gospel?

— Day Three —

> "NEVERTHELESS I HAVE THIS
> AGAINST YOU, THAT YOU HAVE
> LEFT YOUR FIRST LOVE."
> REVELATION 2:4

I remember the first time I held my newborn daughter in my arms. I was a young man, scared and excited as I set off on a new adventure. In an instant, my world changed.

I also remember the nervousness of preaching my first message. And the first time I preached at a small outreach in Canada. And the first time I walked into the Billy Graham Evangelistic Association headquarters after I began working with the ministry full-time. In each of these "first" situations, I was energized and filled with excitement.

It's interesting, though, that this excitement can wear off over time. You can still love something or somebody, but your passion begins to wane as you become comfortable. In Revelation 2, Jesus admonished the church at Ephesus for this very thing. They had lost the *passion* that had first gripped them and driven them to serve God and others.

The same might be said about us. We may be floating through life with the hope of eternity but without the passion of the Savior. We may get more excited about a mundane building project than we do about the peace that passes all understanding.

Today, I ask you to remember your first love. Remember when you surrendered your life to Christ—and rekindle that relationship with Him.

What are your favorite "firsts" in life? How have they changed and defined your journey?

When did you surrender your life to Christ? What changed in you that day? How can you reawaken that hunger you first felt for Him?

What are some ways that you—like the believers in Ephesus— have been "going through the motions" and serving God out of habit rather than passion? What is the remedy for this kind of complacency?

Have you ever had the blessing of meeting a new believer and seeing the spark of passion and hope ignited within him or her? If so, how has that motivated you to share the gospel with others so they too can find the joy of Jesus?

— *Day Four* —

FOR AS THE BODY IS ONE AND HAS
MANY MEMBERS, BUT ALL THE MEMBERS
OF THAT ONE BODY, BEING MANY, ARE
ONE BODY, SO ALSO IS CHRIST.
1 CORINTHIANS 12:12

During a campaign in Europe, my grandfather was given a painting by the local people. At first glance, it just looks like a man in traditional peasant clothing casting seed into a field. But when you look more closely, you see that the farmer has the likeness of my grandfather. Also, there is another man behind a plow, breaking up the soil. And on the edge of the field is a little church.

The painting, in fact, is a parable. My grandfather is the evangelist, sowing the seed. The man behind the plow is breaking the ground so the seed can land in fertile soil. And the church is there to prepare the way for the proclamation of the gospel.

This is very much a picture of us as followers of Christ. As Paul explains in 1 Corinthians 12, we may be different parts of the anatomy, but we are all one body. Some of us are evangelists. Others are teachers. We also have chaplains, prayer warriors, and those who are gifted in working with their hands. As one body, we are diverse—but we all need each other.

Regardless of which part of the body you are, strive to work with the other believers around you. As you do, you will be helping to reach a lost and dying generation for Jesus.

What are your spiritual gifts?

How are you working with other parts of the body of Christ to spread the hope and love of Jesus?

How is your church preparing the way for the proclamation of the gospel in your community? What more can be done to reach those who are lost?

What are your thoughts on "plowing the field," understanding the importance of living and sharing your faith even if you're not the one who "reaps the harvest"?

— *Day Five* —

"MY GRACE IS SUFFICIENT FOR
YOU, FOR MY STRENGTH IS MADE
PERFECT IN WEAKNESS."
2 CORINTHIANS 12:9

I stood in the pulpit, shaking from fever and chills. I had just returned from a mission trip to Africa, where I had been bitten by some sort of tick and contracted a wrenching illness. To make matters worse, a friend of mine—who had graciously agreed to lead worship that day—had lost track of time and continued for fifty-five minutes of our hour-long service!

Clutching the pulpit, I decided to postpone my prepared sermon and struggle through a few minutes about our work in Africa. At the end, I offered an altar call. Immediately, a husband and wife moved to the front, saying they had decided to accept Jesus as their Savior!

As a minister and an evangelist, I often fall into the trap of thinking I need to do everything—prepare the best sermon, preach eloquently, and choose just the right passage. But the fact of the matter is that our best isn't good enough if God isn't at work. Further, He can and will work through us even if we are at our lowest points.

I have actually found that God finds joy in "showing up" when we are out of strength . . . which only serves to illustrate our complete dependence on Him.

Has God ever used you in spite of your own weakness? Has He ever "shown up" when you were out of strength?

It's easy to get frustrated when things aren't working in the way we expect. How can you have "eyes to see" that the Holy Spirit may be working even when your plans fail?

The husband and wife didn't respond because of my preaching but because God was softening their hearts before they even came to church. Could He be doing the same in your sibling, coworker, or child? If so, what steps is He leading you to take?

Compare your brokenness and weakness to God's strength and sovereign plan. Which do you think is more powerful? Can He still work through you today?

LEADER'S GUIDE

---∞---

*T*hank you for your willingness to lead your group through this study! What you have chosen to do is valuable and will make a great difference in the lives of others. The rewards of being a leader are different from those of participating, and we hope that as you lead you will find your own walk with Jesus deepened by this experience.

Redeemed is a five-session study built around video content and small-group interaction. As the group leader, just think of yourself as the host of a dinner party. Your job is to take care of your guests by managing all the behind-the-scenes details so that when everyone arrives, they can just enjoy time together.

As the group leader, your role is not to answer all the questions or reteach the content—the video and this study guide will do most of that work. Your job is to guide the experience and cultivate your small group into a kind of teaching community. This will make it a place for members to process, question, and reflect—not receive more instruction.

Before your first meeting, make sure everyone in the group gets a copy of the study guide. This will keep everyone on the same page and help the process run more smoothly. If some group members are unable to purchase the guide, arrange it so that people can share the resource with other group members. Giving everyone access to all the material will position this study to be as rewarding an experience as possible. Everyone should feel free to write in his or her study guide and bring it to group every week.

SETTING UP THE GROUP

You will need to determine with your group how long you want to meet each week so you can plan your time accordingly. Generally, most groups like to meet for either 60 minutes or 90 minutes, so you could use one of the following schedules:

Section	60 minutes	90 minutes
WELCOME (members arrive and get settled)	5 minutes	5 minutes
SHARE (discuss one or more of the opening questions for the session)	5 minutes	10 minutes
READ (discuss the questions based on the Scripture reading for the week)	5 minutes	10 minutes
WATCH (watch the teaching material together and take notes)	20 minutes	20 minutes
DISCUSS (discuss the Bible study questions you selected ahead of time)	20 minutes	35 minutes
PRAYER / RESPOND (pray together as a group and dismiss)	5 minutes	10 minutes

As the group leader, you'll want to create an environment that encourages sharing and learning. A church sanctuary or formal classroom may not be as ideal as a living room, because those locations can feel formal and less intimate. No matter what setting you choose, provide enough comfortable seating for everyone, and, if possible, arrange the seats in a semicircle so everyone can see the video easily. This will make transition between the video and group conversation more efficient and natural.

Also, try to get to the meeting site early so you can greet participants as they arrive. Simple refreshments create a welcoming atmosphere and can be a wonderful addition to a group study evening. Try to take food and pet allergies into account to make your guests as comfortable as possible. You may also want to consider offering childcare to couples with children who want to attend. Finally, be sure your media technology is working properly. Managing these details up front will make the rest of your group experience flow smoothly and provide a welcoming space in which to engage the content of *Redeemed*.

STARTING THE GROUP TIME

Once everyone has arrived, it's time to begin the group. Here are some simple tips to make your group time healthy, enjoyable, and effective.

First, remind the group members to put their phones on silent. This is a way to make sure you can all be present with one another and with God. Next, give each person a few minutes to respond to the questions in the "Share" and "Read" sections. This won't require as much time in session one, but beginning in session two, people will need more time to share their insights from their personal studies. Usually, you won't answer the discussion questions yourself, but you should go first with the "Share" and "Read" questions, answering briefly and with a reasonable amount of transparency.

At the end of session one, invite the group members to complete the between-sessions personal studies for that week. Explain that you will be providing some time before the video teaching next week for anyone to share insights. Let them know sharing is optional, and it's no problem if they can't get to some of the between-sessions activities some weeks. It will still be beneficial for them to hear from the other participants and learn about what they discovered.

LEADING THE DISCUSSION TIME

Now that the group is engaged, it's time to watch the video and respond with some directed small-group discussion. Encourage all the group members to participate in the discussion, but make sure they know they don't have to do so. As the discussion progresses, you may want to follow up with comments such as, "Tell me more about that," or, "Why did you answer that way?" This will allow the group participants to deepen their reflections and invite meaningful sharing in a non-threatening way.

Note that you have been given multiple questions to use in each session, and you do not have to use them all or even follow them in order. Feel free to pick and choose questions based on either the needs of your group or how the conversation is flowing. Also, don't be afraid of silence. Offering a question and allowing up to thirty seconds of silence is okay. It allows people space to think about how they want to respond and also gives them time to do so.

As group leader, you are the boundary keeper for your group. Do not let anyone (yourself included) dominate the group time. Keep an eye out for group members who might be tempted to "attack" folks they disagree with or try to "fix" those having struggles. These kinds of behaviors can derail a group's momentum, so they need to be steered in a different direction. Model active listening and encourage everyone in your group to do the same. This will make your group time a safe space and create a positive community.

The group discussion leads to a closing time of prayer and individual reflection. Take a few moments to pray as a group, and then encourage the participants to review what they've learned and write down their thoughts to the "Respond" section. This will help them cement the big ideas in their minds as you close the session.

Thank you again for taking the time to lead your group. You are making a difference in the lives of others and having an impact on the kingdom of God.

ABOUT THE AUTHOR

—◦◇◦—

*W*illiam Franklin Graham IV (Will) is the third generation of Grahams to proclaim the gospel of Jesus Christ
under the banner of the Billy Graham Evangelistic Association.
Will is the grandson of Billy Graham and the oldest son of
Franklin Graham.

The first of Will's crusade-style-events—called Celebrations—
took place in 2006 in Leduc, Alberta, Canada. His first cele-
bration on United States soil came later that year in Gastonia,
North Carolina. Since then he has held evangelistic outreaches
on six continents around the world.

In addition to his evangelistic outreaches, Will also serves
as vice president of the Billy Graham Evangelistic Association
and as executive director of the Billy Graham Training Center
at The Cove in Asheville, North Carolina.

Will graduated from Liberty University in 1997 with a bach-
elor of science degree in religion and in 2001 from Southeastern
Baptist Theological Seminary with a master of divinity degree.
Will and his wife, Kendra, have two daughters, Christine Jane
(CJ) and Rachel Austin, and a son, William Franklin V (Quinn).